The Next Chapter
of Your *Life*

Blue Mountain Arts®

New and Best-Selling Titles

By Susan Polis Schutz:

*To My Daughter with Love
on the Important Things in Life*

To My Grandchild with Love

To My Son with Love

~

By Douglas Pagels:

*Always Remember How Special
You Are to Me*

For You, My Soul Mate

The Next Chapter of Your Life

Required Reading for All Teenagers

*Simple Thoughts That Can Literally
Change Your Life*

You Are One Amazing Lady

~

By Wally Amos, with Stu Glauberman:

*The Path to Success Is Paved
with Positive Thinking*

~

By Minx Boren:

Friendship Is a Journey

Healing Is a Journey

By Marci:

Angels Are Everywhere!

Friends Are Forever

10 Simple Things to Remember

To My Daughter

To My Granddaughter

To My Mother

To My Sister

To My Son

You Are My "Once in a Lifetime"

~

By Debra DiPietro:

Short Morning Prayers

~

By Carol Wiseman:

Emerging from the Heartache of Loss

~

By Latesha Randall:

The To-Be List

~

By Dr. Preston C. VanLoon:

The Path to Forgiveness

Anthologies:

A Daybook of Positive Thinking

Dream Big, Stay Positive, and Believe in Yourself

God Is Always Watching Over You

Hang In There

The Love Between a Mother and Daughter Is Forever

Nothing Fills the Heart with Joy like a Grandson

A Son Is Life's Greatest Gift

There Is Nothing Sweeter in Life Than a Granddaughter

There Is So Much to Love About You... Daughter

Think Positive Thoughts Every Day

Words Every Woman Should Remember

You Are Stronger Than You Know

The Next Chapter of Your *Life*

*Thoughts about changes
and new beginnings*

Edited by Douglas Pagels

Blue Mountain Press™
Boulder, Colorado

Copyright © 2013, 2018 by Blue Mountain Arts, Inc.

Library of Congress Control Number: 2012917479
ISBN: 978-1-68088-279-7 (previously ISBN: 978-1-59842-705-9)

Acknowledgments appear on page 92.

Printed in China.
First printing of this edition: 2018

✪ This book is printed on recycled paper.

This book is printed on paper that has been specially produced to be acid free (neutral pH) and contains no groundwood or unbleached pulp. It conforms with the requirements of the American National Standards Institute, Inc., so as to ensure that this book will last and be enjoyed by future generations.

Blue Mountain Arts, Inc.

P.O. Box 4549, Boulder, Colorado 80306

Contents

The next chapter
of your life...
what is it going to be like?

It isn't always easy to make changes, but there's no better advice than this: just do your best. Make sure you stay strong enough to move ahead, because there are some wonderful rewards waiting for you.

It won't all make sense right away, but I promise you: over the course of time, answers will come, decisions will prove to be the right ones, and the path will be easier to see. Here are some things you can do that will help to see you through...

You can have hope. Because it works wonders for those who have it. You can be optimistic. Because people who expect things to turn out for the best often set the stage to receive a beautiful result.

You can put things in perspective. Because some things are important, and others are definitely not.

You can remember that beyond the clouds, the sun is still shining. You can meet each challenge and give it all you've got.

You can count your blessings. You can be inspired
to climb your ladders and have some nice, long
talks with your wishing stars. You can be strong and
patient. You can be gentle and wise.

And you can believe in happy endings. Because you
are the author of the story of your life.

— Douglas Pagels

Every morning, upon awakening, each of us is given a gift... a gift of 24 hours, 1,440 minutes, and more than 86,000 seconds! Before jumping up to begin your rush to get out the door... take just one of those precious moments to think about how you will spend the rest of the day.

24 hours a day, 7 days a week, 52 weeks a year... today, tomorrow, or next week... *it's always the right time to make a change.*

— The Staff at Speaking of Women's Health

Regardless of where you are now or where you've been, you can turn the page and begin again... making the most of all the opportunities that come your way. And rather than just having minutes in the day, you can have moments in time... when your life is what you want it to be... and your tomorrows just shine.

— Douglas Pagels

Do your best
and move ahead,
because there are some
wonderful rewards
waiting for you.

❦

Welcome... to the rest of your life. It's a life full of amazing adventures, should you choose them. You no longer have to settle for less than you deserve.

— Lisa Steadman

You are such a deserving person, much more so than you give yourself credit for being. There are many, many things you do for everyone else. So please, do this one thing for yourself: the next time you picture your future, take the time to brush up on your wishing skills and imagine what a joyful, fulfilling tomorrow looks like… for you.

Don't just color in a paint-by-numbers image of what you're "expected" to be. Come up with a picture that truly reflects your down-to-the-core desires and your most-hoped-for goals. Make it a masterpiece that shows you with a big smile on your face as you take steps on the path that leads in the direction of your dreams. And use that beautiful image to inspire you to make your life more of what you want it to be.

Do it because this is exactly what you would want for someone else. And do it because you deserve the same considerate, wonderful wish… for yourself.

— Douglas Pagels

The result of making the next chapter of your life
the best chapter of your life: so much happiness!

— Douglas Pagels

I like the person I see in the mirror every morning. She smiles at me.

— Judy Gehrke

You can think and live so that your thoughts and actions attract serendipity the way putting out a bird feeder attracts robins and cardinals. You will never again look at some woman who seems to have everything and think, wistfully or enviously, "She leads a charmed life." You'll be too involved in living a charmed life of your own.

— Victoria Moran

Answers will come and decisions will prove to be the right ones.

❧

Get in the habit of noticing what you want.... Most people find that when they have enough joy, their life is filled with abundance. I guarantee that somewhere inside you, you already know what it is you need and want. If anything at all were possible, how would you live your life?

— Dr. Christiane Northrup

I think that life is a series of learning experiences. It's full of questions. And when you find the answers to some of them it's so fulfilling.

— Drew Barrymore

We hold the answer not in our hands but in our hearts.

— Judith Couchman

Being in touch with your heart rather than trying to follow your head is the true guide to a happy life…

Let your heart guide you in how you fill your days… like the wind fills the sails of a boat.

Today I pause in silence several times a day, touch my heart, and look up at the sky.

I like to check in with my heart frequently and make sure I am happy.

My heart is my GPS to help me navigate my life.

It never fails to guide me.

— Michael Gates Gill

You must do what you love. You must do what your heart tells you to do. It's really that simple. When you connect with the things that you love, your spirit just flies. That is what you are supposed to be doing.

— Zoe Elton

I urge you precisely as I urge myself: Reach for your deepest joys. Heed what you genuinely need and value, here and now. Strengthen your good judgment, your discernment, so that you — and those you love — profit from the risks you take.... Bit by intelligible bit, make choices that honor your healthiest instincts, your noble desires. This is how we build a life.

— Marsha Sinetar

Our heads may have an agenda and a plan, but the blueprint for our lives is encoded in our hearts and souls.

— Melody Beattie

Life is a do-it-yourself project, so just do it.

— Mamie McCullough

Do you dare to dream? Do you dare to desire? Do you dare to let your imagination... run to the winds of fancy? What do you want? What do you dearly, truly want?

— Lynn Grabhorn

Most of us don't know what we want. We live our whole lives doing what we think we should want or what we think other people want us to do, and then when we realize we haven't lived our dreams, we have regrets....

Ask yourself the question, "What do I want?"...

Write down whatever it is. A greenhouse, a better relationship with your mother, financial security, world peace. Do it every day for a week, then take that list and cross off everything on that list that isn't what you want.

Cross off what your mother wants, what your father wants, what your other relatives want, what your spouse wants, what your neighbor wants, what the other people in your profession want, so that the only thing you have left is what you want. Once you know what it is, then you can make plans to get it.

Make a treasure map with you at the beginning and what you want at the end.

— Jennifer James, PhD

Over time, the path will be easier to see.

❧

People spend more time planning for a vacation than they do planning for what they want in life. To effectively plan for success, you must be clear about your long-range goals, map a route to reach them, set short-term goals, and schedule time to pursue them.

— Connie Palladino, PhD

I am here to remind you that, if you look closely, there are bread crumbs along the path so that you will know that others, too, have traveled it and survived.

— Vickie Girard

Step by step, every day brings you closer to the good things that you seek and the good that is seeking you.

— Ruth Beckford

Tucked away in a secret corner of our hearts is that college degree or those music lessons or that business to start or that mountain to climb or that book to write. They are all being put off until... someday. When you pursue your dreams, you tap into an unlimited source of energy and enthusiasm. When you don't pursue your dreams, there is a sadness and a sense of "I wonder what would have happened if I had..."

— Rita Emmett

Try to live your life in such a way that whenever you stop and look back at the footprints you've made, you see a path that you are happy to call your own.

— Mike George

There will never be a better time for you to begin than this very moment. Do it now! Don't procrastinate. Remember the law of inertia: a body at rest tends to stay at rest; a body in motion tends to stay in motion. A basic law of physics is on your side. Even the smallest action can multiply into a driving force.

— Cynthia Kersey

There is no "right" time to begin…. Wherever you are is the perfect place to start.

— Rhonda Britten

Don't wait around for the possible to come to you, create your own possibilities….

Don't wait for things to happen; make them happen yourself.

— Alexandra Stoddard

*Have hope, because it
works wonders
for those who have it.*

It is because change is always possible
that hope is always appropriate.

— Victoria Moran

You're... free to take the journey of a lifetime.
Free to experience life, in its newness, its freshness,
its magic — in a way you never have before....

Set yourself free. Let yourself go on a journey of
love. Take notes. Be present. Experience. Learn.
Love and laugh, and cry when you need to. Rest
when you're tired. Take a flashlight to help you see
in the dark. But most of all, take yourself and go.

— Melody Beattie

It doesn't matter what your financial situation is, what you have achieved so far, how old or young you are, what your environment is, your current lifestyle, your nationality, or your educational level. You can improve everything in your life with a positive attitude, determination, commitment, and doing whatever it takes to make it happen.

— Thomas B. Smith

Whether married, partnered, or single, you can live what you love. You just have to get over the jitters and let the dreams show you the way. Tie your kite to reality... check your gut whenever it says, "Hey, wait"... take action when the time is right... remember and treasure what life shows you... but don't ever stand in the way of what you really love.

— Bob and Melinda Blanchard

Everything worth really doing or having requires that we move forward in new directions, take courageous risks, release and let go of our fears... that we open our hearts fully... enter the space of openness to new possibilities... and allow our courage to come forth and override our fear.

— Caroline Joy Adams

What I like most about change is that it's a synonym for "hope." If you are taking a risk, what you are really saying is "I believe in tomorrow and I will be a part of it."

— Linda Ellerbee

When it's time for a new beginning…
You need faith. That things will be better.
You need strength,
   and you'll find it within.
You need patience and persistence.
You need hope, and you need to keep
   it close to the center of everything
   that means the most to you.

You need to put things in perspective.
So much of your life lies ahead!
You need to know how good it can be.

You need to take the best of what
   you've learned from the old and
   bring it to the beautiful days of
   a new journey.

Life's new beginnings happen for very
   special reasons.
When it's time to move on, remember
   that it really is okay.
Because when a new beginning unfolds
   in the story of your life, you go
   such a long way toward making the
   dreams of your tomorrows come true.

— Douglas Pagels

It sounds corny, but I really and truly believe that it's never too late to go after what you want. As the latest of the late bloomers, I'm proof of that.

— Dixie Carter

Many people think it's corny to keep talking about dreams. But if you don't dare to dream, you'll just get the status quo — same old, same old. You may be somewhat safe, but you may be sorry too.

— John Fuhrman

I have learned these past few years that you can't place security over happiness. I look forward to creating my most abundant years living out who I truly am, and doing it with gratitude.

— Sarah Ban Breathnach

Be optimistic...
people who expect things
to turn out for the best
set the stage for great results!

❧

If you're passionate, committed, and willing to believe in yourself, anything is possible. It all starts when you take that half certainty, mix it with your intuition, and jump in.

— Mark Burnett

I'm drawn to stories of overcomers… they seem to have something extra: the ability to lead ordinary lives in extraordinary ways. I believe their secret lies in the attitude they maintain about life, one made of faith, humor, courage, and purpose. They've learned how to juggle lots of balls in the air while keeping both feet on the ground and not toppling over when a strong wind blows.

— Luci Swindoll

Take small but meaningful steps in the right direction. Everything that brings you closer to where you want to end up is good. It's more important to do *something* than to do something perfect. Keep trying different things until you get it.

— Mira Kirshenbaum

If you expect perfection, you'll always be disappointed. But if you create realistic expectations from the beginning, you'll be thrilled to find out that the glass isn't partly empty, it's nearly full.

— Al Trellis and Paul Sharp

Life does not have to be perfect to be wonderful.

— Annette Funicello

Although it takes tremendous courage to change old thought patterns, we can help ourselves do so by adopting the little engine's phrase, "I think I can, I think I can," when we feel helpless or overwhelmed. Keeping our self-talk empowering, not panic producing, helps us do what we want to do and enhances our peace of mind immeasurably.

— Sue Patton Thoele

Wherever you are now, and wherever you want to go, I promise you — someone else has made that journey, and you can make it too.

— David Bach

In the story of *The Little Engine That Could*, whenever faced with a big challenge, the little engine told herself, *I think I can, I think I can, I think I can.* Now that's my kind of choo-choo.

— Ellen Miller

In the end, it's not the years in your life that count.
It's the life in your years.

— Abraham Lincoln

Put things in perspective,
because some things
are important and
others are definitely not.

❧

Give your attention to what's coming instead of what's not here. Once you are comfortable doing that, by the powers that be and the power that you are, you will begin to live the life you came here to live. You will be fulfilling your reason for being.

— Lynn Grabhorn

So much of our lives requires a delicate balancing act. Juggling work and home life. Juggling friends and responsibilities. Juggling our personal needs with the needs of our families.

— Nora Isaacs

Every to-do list you make helps you plan your actions, which in turn helps you use your time better, which, in the end, determines the path your life will follow. The items on your to-do list tend to fall into one of two categories: maintenance or enrichment...

Maintenance jobs are those that are necessary to keep your life running smoothly... cooking, cleaning, mowing the lawn, paying bills, doing the laundry.

Enrichment activities, whether short- or long-term, are those you do by choice, not because you "should" do them. I like the word *enrichment*. You usually know if you've done something enriching because it makes your life seem — well — richer...

The trick is to learn to sandwich the joyful things you *want* to do between the important things you *have* to do.

— Rita Emmett

You don't have to change yourself to change your life.

— Barbara Sher

Maybe this isn't the right time of your life to chase that dream. But maybe — just maybe — you could find some time if you decided to....

When you start to make a list of all the little tasks involved, you may find that at least one task is manageable at this time in your life....

Take a look at your dream. Write a list of the small steps it would take to get started. Then search for ways to find more time to make your dream a reality.

— Rita Emmett

All you can do is all you can do, but all you can do is enough.

— A. L. Williams

Remember that beyond the clouds, the sun is still shining.

❧

Move on so that you can have the wonderful, fulfilling life that you were intended to have.... Finally, once and for all, let the sun come out in your life.

— Joyce L. Vedral, PhD

I have always been delighted at the prospect of
a new day, a fresh try, one more start, with perhaps
a bit of magic waiting somewhere behind the morning.

— J. B. Priestley

The morning sunlight serves as an analogy for a new
beginning. Whatever happened yesterday is gone; the
sunlight spells a new day for new undertakings, new
insights, new resolutions....

It's morning. There's sunlight. There's movement.
There's time.

— Dianna Booher

Maybe now is a good time for us
to take a little journey.

— Vickie Girard

The... program is more than just happy endings. It's also about fearless beginnings. It's about savoring the thrill of a challenge instead of shrinking from it. It's about curiosity and creativity without fear of ridicule or reprisals. It's about having the courage to explore, to change, to grow.... It's about living every moment instead of getting ready to live. It's about the joy of the journey.

— Rhonda Britten

A brief pause for the "tough love" advice...

Starting over, changing paths — however slight the move that we're called to make — isn't easy. Neither is staying defensive, living with our heart closed, betraying ourselves, and pretending nothing is wrong.

— Melody Beattie

We can make ourselves miserable, or we can make ourselves strong. The amount of effort is the same.

— Pema Chödrön

Don't complain if you're not willing to change.

— Natasha Munson

The tragedy of life is not that it ends so soon, but that we wait so long to begin it.

— Author Unknown

Reach for the stars. Immediately, you'll be set apart from other people — the people who didn't decide to make a difference with their lives.

How many more chances will you have? You know, it's a shame how much we take life for granted. We think we're invulnerable; we think we've got all the time in the world.

Not true.

— A. L. Williams

There are only so many tomorrows.

— Michael Landon

Meet each challenge and give it all you've got.

≈

The time has come to reach out and take back the self that stepped aside to make room for the parent, the spouse, the wage earner, the maintenance man, the rescuer, the nurse, the warrior, and the rest of that long list of roles you took on over the years. You need to develop your own thoughts, reawaken your creativity, recover your originality, satisfy your curiosity, and go after all the important things your spirit craved but you never had time for.

— Barbara Sher

This is the only time you'll ever have. You must take it or it will be taken from you.

— Edward M. Hallowell, MD

Ordinary people think merely of spending time. Great people think of using it.

— Author Unknown

Live a life that in the end you can say I loved, I lived, I laughed, I helped, I learned.

— Natasha Munson

We avoid change. We deny what we know in our bones. We block experiences, we ignore intuition, we pass by insight, we avoid transformation. We hold on, afraid to change a pattern even when we are in pain.

When you feel conflict, pain, tension, fear, or confusion, this is a change trying to happen. Don't avoid it or withdraw. Don't turn to busyness or denial. Lean into the feeling, work on the change, take the risk. It will give your life the fullness you seek.

— Jennifer James, PhD

Nobody's life is immune from change. But each change, when guided by awareness, is an opportunity for a better life, and self — a better you — to emerge.

— Laura Day

That old saying about opportunity only knocking once is as archaic as the flat-earth theory and as patently untrue. Opportunity knocks all the time — and it rings your doorbell, calls you up, and sends you e-mails.

— Victoria Moran

Most of us have many more opportunities than we can take advantage of. The old saying that opportunity knocks but once is just plain false. Opportunity will knock again and again. If we never answer the door, however, opportunity will eventually go away and knock somewhere else.

You must prepare yourself for opportunity, so that when it does knock, you recognize it, open the door, and invite it in.

— Al Trellis and Paul Sharp

Count your blessings.

Count your blessings, not your troubles. You'll make it through whatever comes along. Within you are so many answers. Understand, have courage, be strong.

— Douglas Pagels

I can only live in the now of today, but my positive thoughts and actions are helping me create a bright future in which I will enjoy the results.

— Colleen Zuck and Elaine Meyer

Give your future a past to remember.

— Véronique Vienne

It's important to remember that we can live life exuberantly in the present and still keep the future in mind while we do it.

— Nora Isaacs

You don't have to know your future to have one....

It's okay not to know your plans! It really is. In fact, saying "I don't know," instead of pretending you do know, frees you up to consider all kinds of possibilities.

— Danae Jacobson

Every choice we make leads us in one of two directions. We are headed either toward a future that inspires us or toward a past that limits us. When we're moving in the direction of our deepest desires, we feel the support of the entire universe behind us, and we are inspired by our lives. Our excitement wakes us up in the morning and gives us the motivation and energy we need to forge ahead.

— Debbie Ford

Climb your ladders and have some nice, long talks with your wishing stars.

We see all the things we would like to have but don't, all the places we would like to be but aren't, all the ladders we would like to have climbed but didn't.

— Lynn Grabhorn

You need not be discouraged. You can improve your life at any age.

— Tina B. Tessina, PhD

Everyone's life is lived somewhere between their aspirations and their limitations. Truly happy, successful people have limitations, like everyone else, and setbacks that come along on a regular basis.

But what sets them apart from most people is that they're great at making the most of these three things: effort, attitude, and adaptability.

People with smiles in their hearts and success in their lives make the effort to steadily travel in the direction of their dreams; they have an attitude of optimism and appreciation; and they adapt to life by getting out their pens when they need to... and getting to work on a new chapter in their life.

They continually have a hopeful journey to go on, a change they can believe in, and a really good chance to get it right.

— Douglas Pagels

You'll discover that all you need lies within you. You don't have to go to the top of a mountain. You don't have to travel far and wide searching for that certain someone who can touch you with a peacock feather and enlighten you. You don't have to desert your friends and family. You don't even have to get a new job. All you need is your full attention and an attitude of receptivity.

— Sarah Susanka

If the *why* is strong enough,
the *how* becomes easy.

— Laura Stack

Be strong and patient.

❧

When it comes to taking responsibility for your own life, there is no wiggle room, no extra choices for ways to get started.... You either do it or you don't.

— Joyce Meyer

This is your chance to start over and to start stronger. It is your ultimate opportunity to hit the reset button on your life.

— David Bach

Stay present for each step of your journey. We don't go from one place to another in a gigantic leap. We get there in increments, by going through each feeling, each belief, each experience one step at a time.

Sometimes when we pray for miracles, what we're really praying for is help in skipping steps, for shortcuts. The simple act of acceptance, of returning to each step of our path, can often bring us the miracle we need. Then we see the truth. The real miracle is one always available to each of us: it's the miracle of acceptance. We can go where we want to go, one step at a time.

— Melody Beattie

Instead of insisting on hitting a grand slam right away, settle for making it to the ballpark.

— Steve Levinson and Pete C. Greider

For a long time it seemed to me that life was about to begin. But there was always some obstacle in the way, something to get through first, some unfinished business. Only after that would life get under way. At last it dawned on me that these obstacles *were* life.

— Author Unknown

Obstacles keep coming at you. You just have to keep going through them — because it's worth it to do something in your life, as opposed to just fantasizing about doing something.

— Diane Keaton

Behold the turtle; he makes progress only when he sticks his neck out.

— James Bryant Conant

Whatever you do, don't let your progress go unnoticed — even if you are the only one who's noticing.

— Author Unknown

Find some reassurance and comfort in quietly saying this:

I am aware that I am less than some people would prefer me to be, but most people are unaware that I am so much more than what they see.

— Douglas Pagels

I am not a has-been. I'm a will-be.

— Lauren Bacall

All of your decisions from now on can be made in relationship to your road map. If you consider each of your subsequent decisions according to whether it will get you closer to your goal or not, your choices will become more clear and more direct.

— Tina B. Tessina, PhD

The moral of this story is clear: Risk going after what you really want in your life. Give the universe a chance to support you. You won't know until you try.

— Douglas Bloch

"Okay, I'll try" — three little words with unbelievable dividends.

— Luci Swindoll

Be gentle and wise.

At each juncture of "beginning again," we are a little wiser than before, and that modicum of wisdom, learned from experience, makes all the difference. With each step we grow.

— Luci Swindoll

The wise don't expect to find life worth living; they make it that way.

— Author Unknown

Give yourself permission to be in transition.

— Daphne Rose Kingma

Pack your bags. Get out your map.... Go where your heart leads. Your soul knows the way. It will speak quietly through the voice of your heart, your wisdom, your intuition.

— Melody Beattie

Life always offers you a second chance.
It's called "tomorrow."
— Author Unknown

I now have an inner knowing that... I can survive, and even thrive once again. This has brought me to a place of openness to all possibilities — which feels like a fine place to be. For the journey of life really is a mysterious and magnificent adventure, and a new chapter in our lives, one brimming with infinite possibilities, is before us at every moment, just waiting to unfold.

— Caroline Joy Adams

A charmed life is an exuberant life. You get one by loosening up, lightening up, and inviting in stimulating events and people. Helen Keller said… "Life is either a daring adventure, or nothing." Thank you, Helen.

— Victoria Moran

One final note: As you move on with your fabulous life, it's important to remember that it's not always going to be easy. From time to time, you will have setbacks in living and loving your life as it is right now. When you need to, revisit this book for a refresher course in whatever you're struggling with.... Above all else, remember this: Be patient with your progress. Give yourself cocoon time as needed. Then when you're ready, pick yourself up, dust yourself off, and get back in the game.

— Lisa Steadman

And believe in
happy endings, because you
are the author of
the story of your life.

❧

You can start from now and make a brand-new ending. Now is the time to lay that groundwork for a new future. I know you can do it.

— Jim Karas

I feel like a whole new chapter of my life is about to be written, Alice, and this time with a four-color pen.

— Sally Forth

Acknowledgments

We gratefully acknowledge the permission granted by the following authors and authors' representatives to reprint poems or excerpts from their publications: National Speaking of Women's Health Foundation and Dianne Dunkelman for "Every morning, upon…" from IT'S THE RIGHT TIME TO TAKE A PLEDGE FOR WOMEN'S HEALTH: THE BOOK. Copyright © 2006 by National Speaking of Women's Health Foundation. All rights reserved. Polka Dot Press, an imprint of Adams Media, an F+W Publications Company, for "Welcome… to the rest of your life" and "One final note…" from IT'S A BREAKUP NOT A BREAKDOWN by Lisa Steadman. Copyright © 2007 by Lisa Steadman. All rights reserved. Celestial Arts, a division of Random House, Inc., for "Everything worth really doing…" and "I now have an inner knowing…" from A WOMAN OF WISDOM: HONORING AND CELEBRATING WHO YOU ARE by Caroline Joy Adams. Copyright © 1999 by Caroline Joy Adams. All rights reserved. More® Books, an imprint of Meredith® Books, for "I like the person I see…" by Judy Gehrke, "I have learned these past few years…" by Sarah Ban Breathnach, and "Obstacles keep coming at you" by Diane Keaton from 50 CELEBRATE 50: FIFTY EXTRAORDINARY WOMEN TALKING ABOUT FACING, TURNING, AND BEING FIFTY by Connie Collins. Copyright © 2002 by Meredith Corporation. All rights reserved. HarperCollins Publishers for "You can think and live…," "It is because change is…," "That old saying about…," and "A charmed life is an…" from CREATING A CHARMED LIFE by Victoria Moran. Copyright © 1999 by Victoria Moran. All rights reserved. And for "Our heads may have an agenda…" and "Starting over, changing paths…" from FINDING YOUR WAY HOME: A SOUL SURVIVOR KIT by Melody Beattie. Copyright © 1998 by Melody Beattie. All rights reserved. And for "Most of us don't know…" and "We avoid change" from SUCCESS IS THE QUALITY OF YOUR JOURNEY: EXPANDED EDITION by Jennifer James, PhD. Copyright © 1986 by Jennifer James. All rights reserved. And for "Don't wait around for…" from THE ART OF THE POSSIBLE by Alexandra Stoddard. Copyright © 1996 by Alexandra Stoddard. Used by permission of Brandt & Hochman Literary Agents, Inc. All rights reserved. And for "You're… free to take…," "Stay present for each step…," and "Pack your bags" from JOURNEY TO THE HEART by Melody Beattie. Copyright © 1996 by Melody Beattie. All rights reserved. And for "Every choice we make…" from THE RIGHT QUESTIONS by Debbie Ford. Copyright © 2003 by Debbie Ford. All rights reserved. Rizzoli International Publications, Inc., for "Get in the habit of noticing…" by Dr. Christiane Northrup and "I think that life is…" by Drew Barrymore from WOMEN TO WOMEN: A NEW PLAN FOR SUCCESS AND WELL-BEING FROM TODAY'S MOST CELEBRATED WOMEN by Christina Lessa. Copyright © 2000 by Christina Lessa. All rights reserved. Multnomah Books, a division of Random House, Inc., for "We hold the answer…" from DESIGNING A WOMAN'S LIFE: DISCOVERING YOUR UNIQUE PURPOSE AND PASSION by Judith Couchman. Copyright © 1995 by Judy C. Couchman. All rights reserved. And for "You don't have to know…" from THINGS I'VE LEARNED LATELY by Danae Jacobson. Copyright © 2001 by Danae Jacobson. All rights reserved. Gotham Books, an imprint of Penguin Group (USA), Inc., for "Being in touch with your heart…" from HOW TO SAVE YOUR OWN LIFE: 15 LESSONS ON FINDING HOPE IN UNEXPECTED PLACES by Michael Gates Gill. Copyright © 2009 by Michael Gates Gill. All rights reserved. Seal Press, a member of Perseus Books Group, for "You must do what you love" by Zoe Elton and "So much of our lives requires…" and "It's important to remember…" by Nora Isaacs from WOMEN IN OVERDRIVE: FIND BALANCE & OVERCOME BURNOUT AT ANY AGE by Nora Isaacs. Copyright © 2006 by Nora Isaacs. All rights reserved. St. Martin's Press for "I urge you precisely as I urge…" from TO BUILD THE LIFE YOU WANT, CREATE THE WORK YOU LOVE by Marsha Sinetar. Copyright © 1995 by Marsha Sinetar. All rights reserved. Mamie McCullough for "Life is a do-it-yourself project…" from GET IT TOGETHER: AND REMEMBER WHERE YOU PUT IT. Copyright © 1997 by Mamie McCullough & Associates. All rights reserved. Hampton Roads Publishing Co., c/o Red Wheel/Weiser LLC, for "Do you dare to dream?," "Give your attention…," and "We see all the things…" from EXCUSE ME, YOUR LIFE IS WAITING by Lynn Grabhorn. Copyright © 2000 by Lynn Grabhorn. All rights reserved. Connie Palladino, PhD, for "People spend more time planning…" from DEVELOPING SELF-ESTEEM: A GUIDE FOR POSITIVE SUCCESS, REVISED EDITION. Copyright © 1989, 1994 by Crisp Publications, Inc. All rights reserved. Compendium, Inc., for "I am here to remind you…" and "Maybe now is a good time for…" from THERE'S NO PLACE LIKE HOPE by Vickie Girard. Copyright © 2001, 2003 by Vickie Girard and Compendium, Inc. All rights reserved. The Pilgrim Press for "Step by step…" from STILL GROOVIN': AFFIRMATIONS FOR WOMEN IN THE SECOND HALF OF LIFE by Ruth Beckford. Copyright © 1999 by Ruth Beckford. All rights reserved. Walker & Co., a division of Bloomsbury Publishing, Plc, for "Tucked away in a secret corner…," "Every to-do list you make…," and "Maybe this isn't the right time…" from THE PROCRASTINATOR'S HANDBOOK: MASTERING THE ART OF DOING IT NOW by Rita Emmett. Copyright © 2000 by Rita Emmett. All rights reserved. Duncan Baird Publishers Ltd for "Try to live your life…" from 1001 MEDITATIONS: HOW TO DISCOVER PEACE OF MIND by Mike George. Copyright © 2004 by Duncan Baird Publishers Ltd. All rights reserved. Sourcebooks, Inc., for "There will never be a better time…" from UNSTOPPABLE by Cynthia Kersey. Copyright © 1998 by Cynthia Kersey. All rights reserved. Dutton, a division of Penguin Group (USA), Inc., for "There is no 'right' time…" and "The… program is more than…" from FEARLESS LIVING by Rhonda Britten. Copyright © 2001 by Rhonda Britten. All rights reserved. Thomas B. Smith for "It doesn't matter what your financial…" from IF IT IS TO BE IT'S UP TO ME. Copyright © 2001 by Thomas B. Smith. All rights reserved. Sterling Publishing Co., Inc., for "Whether married, partnered, or single…" from LIVE WHAT YOU LOVE: NOTES FROM AN UNUSUAL LIFE by Bob and Melinda Blanchard. Copyright © 2005 by Bob and Melinda Blanchard. All rights reserved. Grand Central Publishing for "What I like most about change…" by Linda Ellerbee and "It sounds corny…" by Dixie Carter from FIFTY ON